ABDO
Publishing Company

DIGESTIVE
System

BODY SYSTEMS

Buddy **BOOKS**
Body Systems

A Buddy Book by **Sarah Tieck**

VISIT US AT
www.abdopublishing.com

Published by ABDO Publishing Company, 8000 West 78th Street, Edina, Minnesota 55439.

Printed in the United States of America, North Mankato, Minnesota.
092010
012011

 PRINTED ON RECYCLED PAPER

Coordinating Series Editor: Rochelle Baltzer
Contributing Editors: Megan M. Gunderson, BreAnn Rumsch, Marcia Zappa
Graphic Design: Jenny Christensen
Cover Photograph: *iStockphoto*: ©iStockphoto.com/PacoRomero.
Interior Photographs/Illustrations: *AP Photo*: Dale Sparks (p. 23); *Eighth Street Studio* (p. 22); *iStockphoto*: ©iStockphoto.com/1001nights (p. 30), ©iStockphoto.com/ aimintang (p. 11), ©iStockphoto.com/andipantz (p. 29), ©iStockphoto.com/artbyjulie (p. 22), ©iStockphoto.com/Calamity_John (p. 17), ©iStockphoto.com/Eraxion (pp. 17, 21), ©iStockphoto.com/FuatKose (p. 23), ©iStockphoto.com/HughStonelan (p. 30), ©iStockphoto.com/killerb10 (p. 25); ©iStockphoto.com/Monkeybusinessimages (p. 5), ©iStockphoto.com/njgphoto (p. 27), ©iStockphoto.com/Photolyric (p. 5), ©iStockphoto.com/sjlocke (p. 13); *Peter Arnold, Inc.*: Ed Reschke (p. 27); *Photo Researchers, Inc.*: Andrew Lambert Photography (p. 9), MedicalRF (p. 7); *Shutterstock*: hkannn (p. 15), Sebastian Kaulitzki (p. 19), Elina Kharichkina (p. 9), Scott Rothstein (p. 9).

Library of Congress Cataloging-in-Publication Data

Tieck, Sarah, 1976-
  Digestive system / Sarah Tieck.
    p. cm. -- (Body systems)
  ISBN 978-1-61613-498-3
  1. Digestive organs--Juvenile literature. 2. Digestive organs--Juvenile literature. I. Title.
  QP145.T52 2011
  612.3--dc22
                              2010019663

Table of Contents

Amazing Body

Your body is amazing! It does thousands of things each day. Your body parts help you eat, move, and grow.

Groups of body parts make up body systems. Each system does important work. The digestive system breaks down food for your body to use. Let's learn more about it!

Your digestive system is mostly located in your middle. But, it starts in your mouth!

Working Together

Eating makes your body work hard! Food travels from your mouth to your throat. From there, it moves into your esophagus and then enters your stomach. Finally, it goes through your small and large intestines.

As you eat, your body digests food. Digestion breaks down food into a usable form. Your body gets rid of what it cannot use. It lets this out as waste.

 How It Sounds

esophagus (ih-SAH-fuh-guhs)
stomach (STUH-muhk)
intestine (ihn-TEHS-tuhn)
digest (DEYE-jehst)

6

YOUR DIGESTIVE SYSTEM

Throat

Esophagus

Stomach

Small Intestine

Large Intestine

Moving Through

Digestion begins in your mouth. Imagine crunching on a carrot. Your tongue and teeth work together to break it down. Your muscular tongue pushes the carrot pieces against your teeth. Your teeth tear, mash, and grind them.

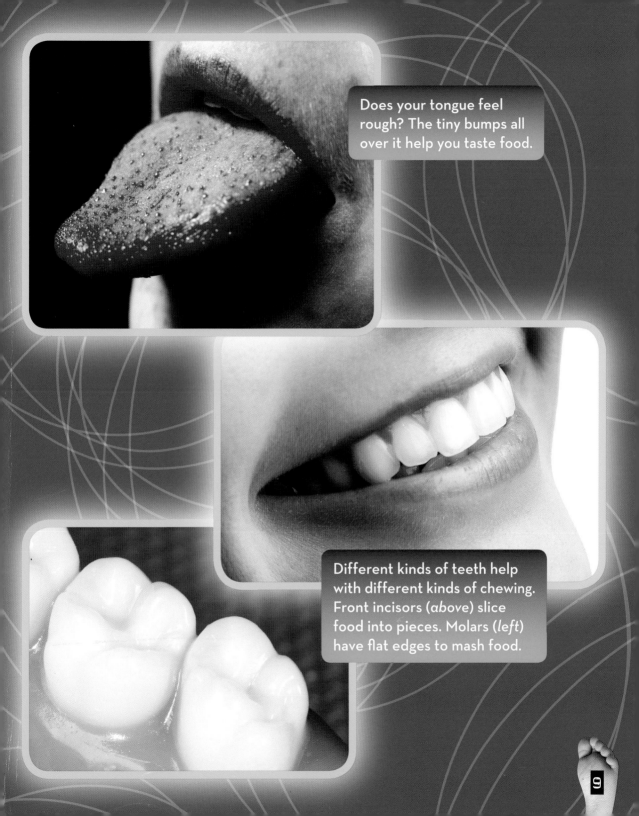

Does your tongue feel rough? The tiny bumps all over it help you taste food.

Different kinds of teeth help with different kinds of chewing. Front incisors (*above*) slice food into pieces. Molars (*left*) have flat edges to mash food.

While your tongue and teeth get to work, your mouth makes a liquid. This liquid is called saliva. It contains an enzyme that breaks down some foods.

Food is in your mouth for a short time. Then, you swallow it. Swallowing is a reflex. Reflexes happen without you even thinking about them.

An enzyme in saliva helps break down bread and rice.

11

Down and Around

As you swallow, food moves from your mouth to your throat. Then, it enters the esophagus. This **muscular** tube pushes food down into your stomach.

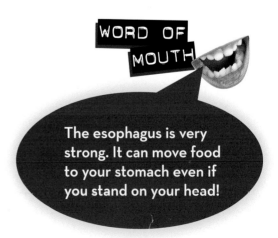

WORD OF MOUTH

The esophagus is very strong. It can move food to your stomach even if you stand on your head!

Parts of your lunch break down in different areas of your digestive system. For example, protein in peanut butter starts to break down in your stomach.

Your stomach is like a bag with very strong muscles. Its walls change size to fit more food. They squeeze and move to break down food.

Stomach walls contain glands. These let out acid and enzymes to help with digestion. Food becomes a thick liquid. When it is ready to leave, muscles relax. They allow the thick liquid to empty into the small intestine.

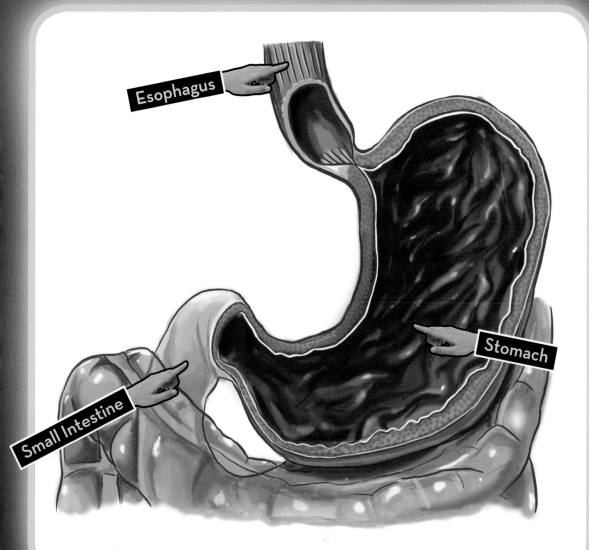

Esophagus

Stomach

Small Intestine

The stomach walls have a protective coating. This keeps them safe from the strong acid inside. Otherwise, the acid would digest your stomach!

Turn, Turn, Turn

When food leaves the stomach, it enters the intestines. These long tubes loop and wind around in your belly.

The intestines have two parts. These are the small intestine and the large intestine. The small intestine is long and narrow. The large intestine is short and wide.

WORD OF MOUTH

An average adult's small intestine is 22 feet (7 m) long. And, a large intestine is 5 feet (2 m) long.

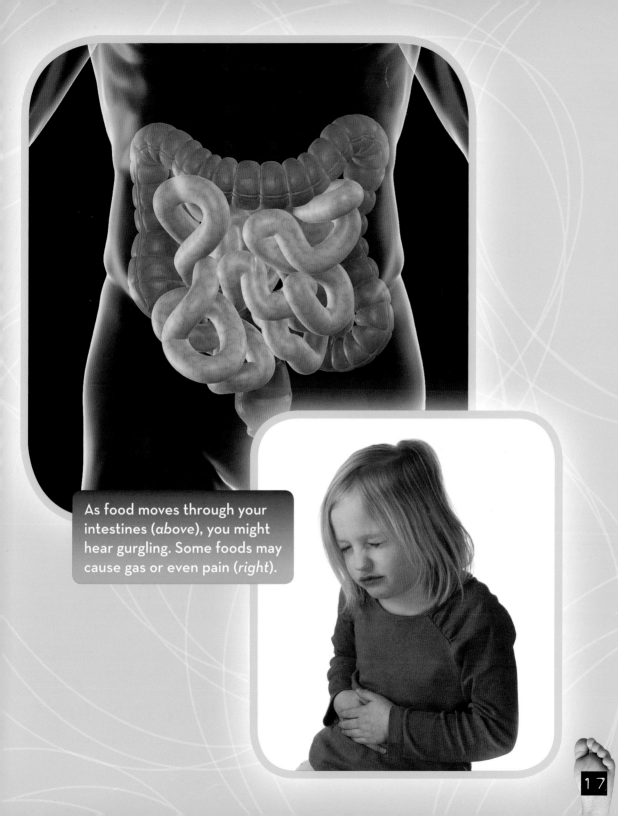

As food moves through your intestines (*above*), you might hear gurgling. Some foods may cause gas or even pain (*right*).

The small intestine has a big job. It is where the most digestion takes place. Enzymes from the small intestine, the liver, and the pancreas help out. Together, they complete the digestion of food.

Tiny bumps called villi line the small intestine. They help your body get nutrients from food. Nutrients soak through the villi and enter the blood. Blood carries nutrients to parts of the body that need them.

How It Sounds

pancreas (PAN-kree-uhs)
villi (VIH-leye)

18

Up close, villi look like tiny fingers.

Last Stop

Your body doesn't use all the parts of the food you eat. The liquid containing the unused parts moves from the small intestine to the large intestine. The unused parts are waste. So, they must leave your body.

The large intestine removes water from the waste. Then, it stores what's left in your rectum until it can be pushed out.

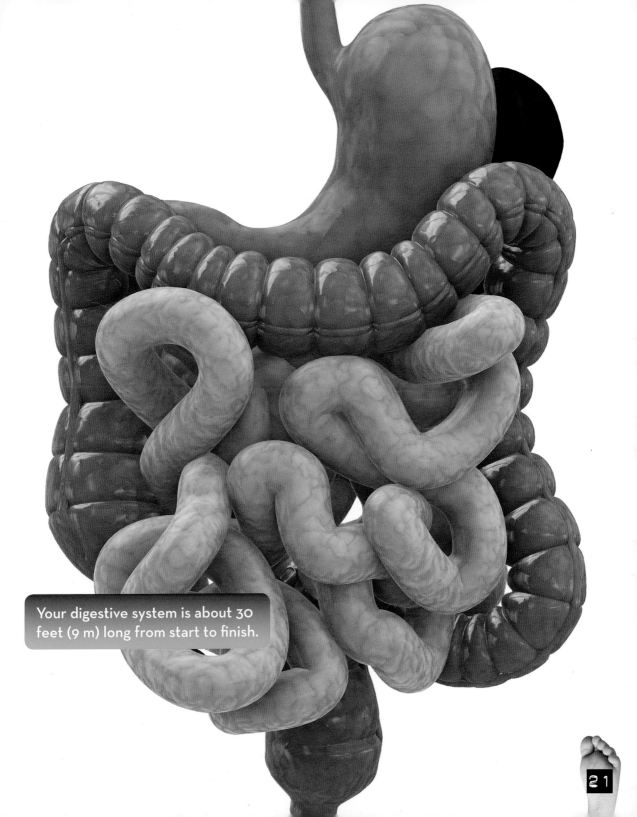

Your digestive system is about 30 feet (9 m) long from start to finish.

Brain Food

How come food doesn't go into your lungs?

The esophagus and the windpipe both connect to your throat. Air goes down the windpipe and into the lungs. When you swallow, a flap covers the windpipe so food goes down the esophagus. This happens without you even thinking about it!

Can food go down the wrong pipe?

Sometimes people swallow wrong. When this happens, they may choke. Doing the Heimlich maneuver (*right*) can remove the food. You may need to ask an adult for help!

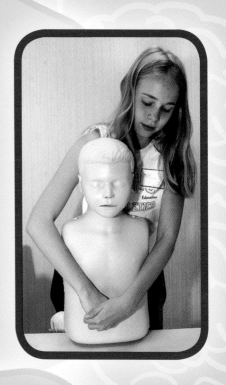

What is a burp?

Gas pushed out of your stomach may come out as a burp. This can happen if you swallow extra air when you eat. It can also come from drinks such as soda, which contain gas. The gas can get trapped in your stomach. A burp lets it out!

Gurgle Gurgle

Eating certain foods, being sick, or feeling worried can upset your digestive system. Your stomach may hurt. You may even throw up or have diarrhea.

Your body needs water more than food. You could only live about a week without water. But, you could survive many weeks without food!

WORD OF MOUTH

24

When you throw up or have diarrhea, your body loses water. Taking in extra liquids, even soup, will help keep water in your body.

25

Often, you can help your digestive system heal. Get plenty of rest. Drink water and eat mild, healthy foods.

Some people may need to see a doctor. Doctors have tools to view the esophagus, the stomach, and the intestines.

Certain X-rays and special cameras let doctors see the stomach and the intestines.

Doctors use otoscopes to look inside the mouth and the throat.

An Important System

Think about how much happens every time you eat. You digest food without even thinking about it!

By learning about your digestive system, you can protect it. Then, you can make good choices to keep your body healthy.

Food gives you energy to move, play, and think. Ask your doctor what the right amount of food is for you to eat. This will help you stay at a healthy weight.

WORD OF MOUTH

Eating fiber helps with digestion. Apples, whole-grain bread, and beans contain fiber.

HEALTHY BODY FILES

DRINK UP

✔ Water helps your body digest food and get rid of waste.

✔ Many doctors suggest drinking eight glasses of water each day.

CLEAN TEETH

✔ Brush your teeth at least twice a day to keep them healthy. Brushing after each meal is best.

✔ Do you eat candy? Be sure to brush extra good. Sugar causes cavities.

✔ Remember to floss! This prevents gum disease.

EAT HEALTHY

✔ Meat, fish, and eggs contain protein. Protein helps your body repair cells.

✔ Bread, pasta, and cereal contain starches. These give you energy.

Important Words

diarrhea (deye-uh-REE-uh) a condition in which a person has loose bowel movements, or poop, that happen often.

enzyme (EHN-zime) something made in living cells of plants and animals. It helps break down food.

gland a body part that makes things the body needs. For example, sweat glands let out sweat to cool the skin.

muscles (MUH-suhls) body tissues, or layers of cells, that help move the body. Something with strong, well-developed muscles is muscular.

nutrient (NOO-tree-uhnt) something found in food that living beings take in for growth and development.

protect (pruh-TEHKT) to guard against harm or danger.

Web Sites

To learn more about the digestive system, visit ABDO Publishing Company online. Web sites about the digestive system are featured on our Book Links page. These links are routinely monitored and updated to provide the most current information available.

www.abdopublishing.com

Index